Supplicatory Canon to Saint Joseph the Hesychast

Anna Skoubourdis

**Published by: Virgin Mary of Australia and Oceania
2021 ©**
oceanitissa@gmail.com
www.oceanitissa.com.au
Youtube: Oceanitissa

Subscribe to receive updates and Orthodox Christian
creative media
www.oceanitissa.com

Troparion of the Venerable One. Tone IV, Spec. Mel. "Swiftly overtake..."

The offspring of Athos and beauty of monastics, a champion of ascesis and haven of stillness art thou shown to be, O our Father. By thy life, thou hast revealed the ways of Grace: by thy prayer, thou hast saved those who faithfully entreat thee; wherefore intercede with the Lord, O Joseph our venerable Father.

Another of the Venerable One. Same Tone.

Having first subdued thy flesh with ascesis, thou didst resolutely lift thy mind from earthly things, O our venerable Father. Thou didst perceive through mystic vision the lands of the saved: thou hast shown them that desire it the path of salvation; wherefore save thou now also those who honour thy memory.

Kontakion. Tone VIII, Spec. Mel. "To thee, the Champion..."

By the streams of thy tears, O Father, thou didst wash clean, and by thy sleepless prayers thou didst make gleam, the garment of thy soul, O Joseph; and within the incorrupt Bridechamber thou dost now exult with the Saints whose way of life thou didst follow. With them, do thou pray that those who honour thee be saved.

Blessed is our God always, now and forever and to the ages of ages. Amen.

Psalm 142

O Lord, hear my prayer, give ear to my supplications in Your truth; hear me in Your righteousness. Do not enter into judgment, with Your servant, for in Your sight no one living is justified. For the enemy has persecuted my soul; he has crushed my life to the ground; he has made me dwell in darkness, like those who have long been dead, and my spirit is overwhelmed within me; my heart within me is distressed. I remembered the days of old; I meditated on all Your works: I pondered on the work of Your hands. I spread out my hands to You; my soul longs for You, like a thirsty land.

Hear me quickly, O Lord; my spirit fails. Do not turn Your face away from me, lest I be like those who go down into the pit. Cause me to hear Your mercy in the morning, for in You I have put my trust. Cause me to know, O Lord, the way in which I should walk, for I lift up my soul to You. Rescue me, lord, from my enemies; to You have I fled for refuge. Teach me to do Your will, for You are my God. Your good Spirit shall lead me in the land of uprightness. For Your name's sake, O Lord, You shall quicken me. In Your righteousness You shall bring my soul out of trouble, and in Your mercy, You shall utterly destroy my enemies. And you shall destroy all those who afflict my soul; for I am Your servant.

Tone 4

God is the Lord and has revealed Himself to us; blessed is He who comes in the name of the Lord.

> *Vs. 1. Give thanks to the Lord for He is good, for His mercy endures forever.*
> *Vs. 2. All the nations have surrounded me, but in the name of the Lord, I have overcome them.*
> *Vs. 3. This has been done by the Lord, and it is wonderful in our eyes.*

Tone 4.

He Who was raised up.

The model and excellence (height) of hesychasm, and the worker of the neptic way of life, you who are excellent/outstanding among the righteous and a great ascetic, cease not guarding your children from every necessity, O Joseph our Father, we pray, and intercede on behalf of our souls to the Master, that He may grant mercy to us.

Glory.

Be quick to anticipate.

Through your former asceticism, you subdued the flesh, you raised the thought your mind on high away from the earthly, O our Venerable Father. Knowing in theory and saving the peoples, you showed to those yearning the way of salvation, therefore, save those who now honour your memory.

Both now.

He Who was raised up.

O Theotokos, we shall never be silent * of your mighty acts, all we the unworthy; * had you not stood to intercede for us * who would have delivered us, from the numerous perils? * Who would have preserved us all * until now with our freedom? * O Lady, we shall not depart from you; * for you always save your servants, from all tribulation. (GOARCH)

Psalm 50

Have mercy on me, O God, according to Your great mercy; and according to the multitude of Your compassion blot out my transgression. Wash me thoroughly from my iniquity and cleanse me from my sin. For I acknowledge my iniquity, and my sin is ever before me. Against You, You only, have I sinned, and done this evil in Your sight, that You may be found just when You speak, and blameless when You are judged. For behold, I was conceived in iniquities, and in sins my mother bore me.

For behold, You have loved truth: You have made known to me the secret things of Your wisdom. You shall sprinkle me with hyssop, and I shall be made clean: You shall wash me, and I shall be whiter than snow. Make me to hear joy and gladness, that bones which You have broken may rejoice. Turn Your face away from my sins and blot out all my iniquities. Create in me a clean heart, O God, and renew a steadfast spirit within me. Do not cast me away from Your presence, and do not take Your Holy Spirit from me. Restore to me the joy of Your salvation: And establish me with Your governing Spirit.

I shall teach transgressors Your ways, and the ungodly shall turn back to You. Deliver me from bloodguiltiness, O God, the God of my salvation, my tongue shall rejoice in Your righteousness. O Lord open my lips, and my mouth shall show forth Your praise. For if You had desired sacrifice, I would give it: You do not delight in burnt offering. A sacrifice to God is a broken spirit, God will not despise a broken and humbled heart.

Do good in Your good pleasure to Sion; and let the walls of Jerusalem be built. Then You shall be pleased with a sacrifice of righteousness, with oblation and whole burnt offerings. Then they shall offer bulls on Your altar.

Ode 1. Plagal of the Fourth Tone
Crossing the waters.

O Saint of God, intercede for us.
In being burdened by all kinds of misfortunes, I flee
unto you, O most compassionate Joseph, and I pray that
through your prayers, my Father, you might deliver me
from sorrow and evils.

O Saint of God, intercede for us.
The assaults of illogical attacks on my soul, O my
Father, Joseph, shake me constantly; therefore in your
stillness, bring peace through your pleasing
intercessions to God.

O Saint of God, intercede for us.
The multitude of my wicked passions overcome me,
and I am clearly to blame; cease their power, through
your compassionate entreaties, most hallowed one.

Most Holy Theotokos, save us.
Theotokion
O Queen of All and gate of God, open to me your
compassion, as the Mother of the Saviour, and deliver
me from every abuse of the enemies who wage war
against me, through your intercessions.

Ode 3.
The apse of the heavens.

O Saint of God, intercede for us.
Through force, you reached the apse of the heavens and
you were illumined with the immaterial light, wholly
shining and withering the dominion of the flesh, and
toward heavens' heights you were exalted, acquiring a
dispassionate nous.

O Saint of God, intercede for us.
Through the shedding of your tears, you extinguished
the passions; therefore, we hymn you with longing,
praying that your divine memory, through your fervent
intercessions O Father, might deliver us from evil and
every assault of the enemy.

Glory.
In the storm of foolishness, we have sinned, O Holy
One, deliver us from this and our terrible passions, we
ask; graciously grant to us the strength to walk towards

divine zeal and virtue, through your entreaties.

Both now.
Theotokion
I, your humble servant, implore you, O Virgin. Do not
abandon me, O Mother, who am estranged by passions
and am being weighed down; but through your
compassion, kindly guide me to divine fear.

Deliver us, * all of your children from dangers, O Holy
Father, * who in faith and love flee ever to you, * and
grant to us your protection.

Turn to me, * in your good favour, all praise-worthy
Theotokos; * look upon my grave illnesses, * which
painfully sting my flesh * and heal the cause of my
soul's pain and suffering.

Kathisma in the Second Tone.

A fervent prayer.
A fervent protector and most noble champion you have
been shown to us who cry out to you with longing and
faithfully call upon you: O Joseph, our father, come to
us and from terrible evils deliver us, since you
unceasingly have presence before the Lord.

Ode 4.
O Lord, I have heard of.

O Saint of God, intercede for us.
Your God-loving way ceases all the weaknesses of the
body, and calms the waves of the soul, through divine
Grace which dwells in you.

O Saint of God, intercede for us.
Grant divine enlightenment, respite, and strength to
those in illness, and the forgiveness of their
transgressions, through your august prayers, O Father.

O Saint of God, intercede for us.
Those who fall down in veneration before your august
dwelling place are granted the healing, which they draw
joyfully and glorify your compassion.

O Saint of God, intercede for us.
Through asceticism, you traversed through the passions
of the flesh in your knowledge, and you became, O
inspired of God, a partaker of the divine Light, just as
you desired.

Most Holy Theotokos, save us.
Theotokion
O Immaculate One, as Ever-Virgin, you became the
dwelling place of the God of All; from Whom you have
shown your servant to be a vessel of divine Grace.

Ode 5.
Lord, enlighten us.

O Saint of God, intercede for us.
Guard us through your intercession, O our Father, and in your presence before the Lord, strike down now the one who tempts us bitterly.

O Saint of God, intercede for us.
Grant to us, through your intercessions, O Blessed one, enlightenment and redemption, that we may prove victorious against all circumstances.

O Saint of God, intercede for us.
Fulfil the requests, O Godly-minded Father, of those who honour your holy memory, O divine Joseph.

Most Holy Theotokos, save us.
Theotokion
We have you as a firm support and sure salvation, O Queen of All, for we are delivered from all misfortunes, O Lady.

Ode 6.
Be merciful unto me.

O Saint of God, intercede for us.

My sins, O Venerable one, have become like a heavy burden and asphyxiate me; deliver me, O inspired of God, through your entreaties in your noble presence before God.

O Saint of God, intercede for us.
As a treasure of support, our Father Joseph, come to
heal my feeble mind; grant to me your grace, just as I
give myself in a pleasing manner to the Lord.

Glory.
Lull the storm of passions, O our Father, from the
dangers of the enemy and every evil, for those who
honour you in faith, through your pleasing intercessions
to the Master.

Both now.
Theotokion
In obligation, I run to your holy temple, and as a pitiful
suppliant, I stand before you, O Lady; accept my tears,
just as Christ the Lord accepted the coins of the widow
of old.

Deliver us, * all of your children from dangers, O Holy
Father, * who in faith and love flee ever to you, * and
grant to us your protection.

Spotless one, * who by a word, did bring to us the Word
eternal, * in the last days ineffably; do you now plead
with him * as the one with the motherly favour.

Kontakion

Tone 2. A protection of Christians.
You appeared as an all-bright star, and an unsleeping
intercessor of your disciples, shining upon those in the
darkened depths of passion, becoming a guide for the
wandering and a leader for monastics for those

imploring you in faith; therefore, reward us with divine Grace, which you received from the Lord, since you are our compassionate Father, O Joseph, us who hymn you.

Prokeimenon.

Tone 4.

Precious in the sight of the Lord is the death of his Saint.

Verse: Blessed is the man who fears the Lord.

The reading is from the holy Gospel according to Matthew (11:27-30)

All things have been handed over to me by my Father; and no one knows the Son except the Father, and no one knows the Father except the Son and anyone to whom the Son chooses to reveal him. "Come to me, all you that are weary and are carrying heavy burdens, and I will give you rest. Take my yoke upon you, and learn from me; for I am gentle and humble in heart, and you will find rest for your souls. For my yoke is easy, and my burden is light."

Tone 2.
Glory to the Father and the Son and the Holy Spirit. Through the intercessions of your Venerable One, Merciful One wash away the multitude of my many personal offences.

Both now and ever and to the ages of ages. Amen.
Through the intercessions of the Theotokos, merciful
One, wash away my many personal offenses.

Verse: *Have mercy upon me, O God, according to Your
great mercy; and according to the multitude of Your
compassions blot out my transgressions.*

Plagal of the 2nd Tone
Having laid all their hope.
Driving away fear and terrible weariness, you walked
the road of life bearing no fear, driving away the many
labours and the heavy burning heat, all in your divine
love. Therefore, just like a hurricane in your life, you
completely burned the beam of the demon who hates
good, O Holy one, just as he appeared and clearly
confessed to you; therefore, save those who hymn you
from his evil, through your prayers.

Ode 7.
Coming out of Judea.

O Saint of God, intercede for us.

In fullness, show our souls the gladness and joy of your
inspiration, O godly-minded Joseph, us who plead you,
and teach us to find the delight of the Prayer, just as you
did.

O Saint of God, intercede for us.
Deliver us from temptation, danger, the madness of the
demons, and every weakness, for those who take

courage in you and ever cry out to you: grant to your children unceasing prayer.

O Saint of God, intercede for us.
I am now enslaved in darkness by every kind of passion, so grant that you brighten me, O Father, as I approach you with yearning, and cry to you: * O the God of our Fathers, blessed are You.

Most Holy Theotokos, save us.
Theotokion
The Creator of humanity dwelt within your womb, O Lady, Queen of All, the protection of humankind, which is being tossed about by storms, therefore, show to us who cry out: make us worthy of your motherly care and protection.

Ode 8.
The King of heaven.

O Saint of God, intercede for us.
Do not overlook those who pray to you for help, O godly-minded one, seeking and requesting your divine protection.

O Saint of God, intercede for us.
Grant your abundant compassion to those who faithfully ask you, my Father, and praise your cloistered life.

O Saint of God, intercede for us.
Through your prayers to the Saviour, turn away your

children from dangers, sorrows, and pain, O Joseph,
blessed of God.

Most Holy Theotokos, save us.
Theotokion
From you was born, Him Who was begotten before the
ages, just as was written from the Father without flow,
therefore, save us, O Mother of God, use who exalt you.

Ode 9.
Saved through you.

O Saint of God, intercede for us.
The streams of my many tears, reject not, as the most
compassionate Father that you are, and grant me
compunction and make me worthy of grace.

O Saint of God, intercede for us.
Become a strength and healing for my soul has been
wounded by my carelessness and stubborn habits, so
that I might glorify you.

Glory.
Through your prayers, loosen the bonds of my
transgressions and tear up the handwriting of my many
sins, since I seek refuge in your divine shelter.

Both now.
Theotokion
O Mistress, do not show me a malignant joy of the
demons in the time of Judgment, O Queen of All, but
through the goodwill of your Son, be compassionate to
me.

Megalynaria.

Truly you are worthy to be blessed, * Mother of our God, the Theotokos, * you the ever blessed one, and all blameless one, * and the Mother of our God. * You are honoured more than the Cherubim, * and you have more glory, * when compared, to the Seraphim; * You, without corruption, * did bear God, the Logos; * You are the Theotokos; * You do we magnify.

In holy glory, O God-bearer, you stand before the throne of our Saviour and God, therefore remember us who celebrate your memory with longing, O All-blessed Joseph, our divine Father.

Through your prayers, save those who piously praise your holy struggle and your toils of reclusion, in their hesychasm and celebrating your memory.

Seek peace from God, the calming of temptations, patience until the end, and the salvation of souls for those who honour you and look to your aid, O Father.

Rejoice, the beauty of Athos, rejoice the most wise healer of monastics, rejoice the divine paradigm of hesychasm, and precise guardian of Holy Tradition.

For the Annunciation of the Theotokos.
Gabriel now proclaims the Good News, crying out with fear, "Rejoice," to Mary; "O, what a strange fashion! For the Creator is held within the womb of the undefiled, to save those whom He fashioned.

For the Holy Sash of the Theotokos.
Priceless sash of the Pure one, the source of miracles, and the treasury of grace, save your servants from every harm, for it is the vessel of life since it girded you.

For the Wonderworking Icons.
I venerate your august icons, the Paramythia (the Comforter), the august Vematarissa (of the Altar), the Antiphonousa (the Answerer), the Pyrobolethesa (the Shot with Arrows), the divine Esphagmene (the Slain), and the Elaiobryti (the Oil Giver).

For the All Holy Lady, the Queen of All.
Being called the Throne of God, you are seated on a throne in your august icon, and you shelter your flock from every kind of danger, O Queen of All, as we sing your magnificence.

The Megalynarion of the church is chanted, then:

With the hosts of Angels, God's messengers, * with the Lord's Forerunner, * and Apostles, the chosen twelve, * with the saints most holy, * and with you, the Theotokos, * we seek your intercession * for our salvation.

Trisagion

Holy God, Holy Mighty, Holy Immortal, have mercy upon us (3).

Glory to the Father and the Son and the Holy Spirit, now and forever and to the ages of ages. Amen.

Most holy Trinity, have mercy upon us; Lord, pardon our sins; Master, forgive our transgressions; Holy One, visit and heal our infirmities, for Your name's sake.

Lord have mercy (3).

Glory to the Father, and the Son and the Holy Spirit, now and forever and to the ages of ages. Amen.

Our Father, Who art in heaven, hallowed be Thy name. Thy kingdom come, Thy will be done, on earth as it is in heaven. Give us this day our daily bread; and forgive us our trespasses as we forgive those who trespass against us. And lead us not into temptation but deliver us from evil. Amen.

Troparion
Fourth Tone. Be quick to anticipate.
The blossom of Athos and the beauty of monastics, you were shown to be the champion of asceticism and the harbour of hesychasm, O our Father, you showed through your life the ways of Grace, and you save those who in faith ask of you, through your prayers. Therefore, intercede to the Lord, O Joseph our Venerable Father.

Glory. Both now.
Theotokion. Troparion of the All Holy Lady, the Queen of All.
The grace-streaming icon of the august Queen of All, save those who fervently seek your grace, O Lady. Save those who run to you from difficult circumstances,

guard your flock from every danger, as we ever call upon your deliverance.

Tone 2

Joseph took You down.

Speedily deliver my from temptation, O Joseph our Father, since you love your children, I implore you, for the enemy wages war against me in vain, the bitter demons come upon me, seeking to snatch the soul of your servant, as a pitiful sparrow; do not overlook me until the end; for you are greatly known to be godly-minded, since you are a refuge for me.

Lady, do you receive, * from your servants, their many prayers; * and deliver all of us, * from all sadness and necessity.

My numerous hopes are placed * before you, most holy One; * Mother of our God, * guard me with care, within your sheltered arms.

Through the prayers of our Holy Fathers, Lord Jesus Christ our God, have mercy on us and save us. Amen.

Biography

Brief biography of St. Joseph the Hesychast from the website of St. Anthony's Monastery in Arizona

Francis Kottis (Saint Joseph's name before his monastic tonsure) was born in Paros on February 12, 1897, the fourth of seven children to the simple but pious couple George and Maria Kottis. Because of their extreme poverty, Francis left home at the age of seventeen to work in Piraeus as a merchant to support his large family. When he was twenty-three years old he was engaged to a pious girl and lived in exemplary chastity, never touching his fiancee for fear of coming to the point of kissing her.

One day he beheld a wondrous vision of two angels in the form of palace guards, leading him to serve the heavenly king. After this vision, he became pensive and lost all interest in worldly things; he spent his time reading the lives of saints, especially those of the great ascetic Fathers, which ignited in his heart the desire to become a monk. He then called off his engagement, and in preparation for his life on the Holy Mountain,3 he started conditioning himself to ascetic struggles by fasting and praying in the countryside of Athens. In 1921, after two years of living ascetically in the world, he finally made his way to the Holy Mountain, his heart longing for a God-bearing spiritual guide to teach him the art of noetic prayer, and he began traversing the crags and caves in search of one. After searching for sometime without success, he decided to join the brotherhood of Saint Daniel of Katounakia. Renowned for his discernment and exalted spiritual life, Saint Daniel chose a moderate ascetical program for his brotherhood. Francis, however, was inclined to a more austere spiritual life and total dedication to unceasing prayer of the heart, which requires great silence and humility, and thus he stood out from the rest of the brotherhood. Saint Daniel knew he could not stay with his brotherhood, but he also knew that Francis needed a companion, a fellow ascetic, in order to avoid delusion. So he told him that until a co-struggler could be found for him, he should cultivate the Jesus Prayer alone in some remote cave, coming to him occasionally for spiritual guidance. One day, after suffering many temptations, he was granted a vision of the uncreated light, and he received the gift of ceaseless prayer. From that point on until his death, the prayer was said in his heart unceasingly, granting him exalted spiritual states and divine visions. Eventually, a suitable co-struggler, Father Arsenios, was sent to him by Saint Daniel. These two spiritual warriors would be inseparable companions for the rest of their lives, leading an austere ascetical life together. In the beginning Father Arsenios regarded Francis as his geronda, even though Father Arsenios had already been tonsured a monk and Francis was still a layman. However, on the Holy Mountain, to be a geronda, you have to be obedient to a geronda until his death.

Therefore, following Saint Daniel's advice they became disciples of two humble old gerondas in Katounakia named Joseph and Ephraim. It was not long before one of them, Saint Joseph, reposed in the Lord. Geronda Ephraim, now their sole geronda, was soon convinced by the exceptional lifestyle of young Francis that this spiritual warrior should be officially enrolled in the angelic monastic order. Thus, the day of his monastic tonsure was set for Sunday, August 31, 1925, the commemoration day of the deposition of the precious sash of the Theotokos. His tonsure took place in the cave of Saint Athanasios the Athonite, and he received the name Joseph, after his reposed geronda. After some years, Geronda Ephraim also fell asleep in the Lord, and the young Father Joseph became a proper geronda. Soon he began attracting monastic aspirants, but few of them were able to endure his severe ascetic program. Eventually, the nucleus of his brotherhood would consist of five disciples: his co-ascetic Father Arsenios; Father Athanasios, his brother in the flesh; Father Joseph the Cypriot, who would later become the geronda of the Holy Monastery of Vatopaidi; Father Ephraim, later abbot of the Holy Monastery of Philotheou and future geronda of thirty-three monasteries in Greece, the US, and Canada, including Saint Anthony's Monastery in Arizona; and Father Haralambos, later abbot of the Holy Monastery of Dionysiou. Also, it is noteworthy to mention Saint Ephraim of Katounakia; although he belonged to a different brotherhood, he was guided spiritually by Saint Joseph, and thus is also considered one of his disciples. In 1938, seeking greater solitude, Saint Joseph and his community moved from Saint Basil's Skete to a cave at Little Saint Anne's, but after 15 years of living in the harsh conditions of Little Saint Anne's, the fathers' health started to deteriorate, and so in 1953, Saint Joseph decided to move the community farther down the mountain, near the sea, to New Skete, where he would spend the last six years of his life. A few months before his death, he was visited by the Virgin Mary, whom he held in special reverence, and was promised by her, that she would take him on her feast day. Thus the saint fell asleep in the Lord, on August 15, 1959, the day the Orthodox Church celebrates the Dormition of the Most Holy Mother of God. Saint Joseph's legacy has been carried on by his disciples, who have reestablished the practice of noetic prayer and watchfulness on the Holy Mountain, brought Athonite monasticism to the United States and Canada, and encouraged many Orthodox faithful through the publishing of his life and letters. Today the spiritual grandchildren of Saint Joseph, who endearingly refer to him as "Pappou Iosif" (Grandfather Joseph in Greek), call upon him to help them in their spiritual life, and he in turn stands before the throne of God and intercedes for his spiritual children and grandchildren, and all those who call upon him.